Introduction

Welcome to "Financial Freedom: A Roadmap to Building Wealth and Passive Income." This e-book aims to equip you with the knowledge and strategies to take control of your finances, invest wisely, and create streams of passive income. Whether you're just starting your financial journey or looking to enhance your existing strategy, this guide will provide actionable steps to achieve your financial goals.

Understanding the Journey to Financial Freedom

Achieving financial freedom is more than just accumulating wealth. It's about making informed decisions that lead to financial stability and independence. This e-book is designed to demystify the complex world of personal finance and investment, offering clear, practical advice that can be tailored to your unique circumstances.

Why Financial Freedom Matters

Financial freedom means having the ability to make life choices without being overly stressed about the financial implications. It provides the security to handle emergencies, the freedom to pursue your passions, and the ability to live a life by design rather than by default.

1. **Security and Peace of Mind**: Financial freedom provides a safety net, reducing anxiety about unexpected expenses or job loss. It ensures that you can maintain your lifestyle even during tough times.

2. **Life Choices**: With financial freedom, you have the flexibility to make significant life choices, such as retiring early, traveling, starting a business, or pursuing hobbies and interests without financial constraints.
3. **Generational Wealth**: Achieving financial freedom allows you to build and transfer wealth to future generations, ensuring their financial stability and opportunities for growth.

Key Components of Financial Freedom

To guide you toward financial freedom, this e-book covers several key components:

1. **Building a Strong Financial Foundation**: Learn how to set financial goals, understand your net worth, and create an emergency fund.
2. **Effective Budgeting and Saving**: Discover practical tips for creating and sticking to a budget, tracking expenses, and saving efficiently.
3. **Debt Management**: Strategies to manage and eliminate debt, freeing up more resources for savings and investments.
4. **Investing Basics and Advanced Strategies**: From understanding the basics of stocks and bonds to exploring advanced investment strategies, this e-book covers it all.
5. **Passive Income Streams**: Explore various ways to generate passive income, including dividends, real estate, and digital products.
6. **Retirement Planning**: Ensure a secure retirement by learning about different retirement accounts, calculating retirement needs, and developing effective withdrawal strategies.
7. **Protecting Your Wealth**: Discover how to protect your wealth through insurance, estate planning, and legal protections.

How to Use This Book

This book is structured to provide a comprehensive guide to financial freedom. Each chapter focuses on a specific aspect of personal finance and investment, with actionable tips and real-life examples to help you apply the concepts.

- **Beginner-Friendly**: If you're new to personal finance, start from the beginning to build a strong foundation.
- **Focused Learning**: If you're looking to improve a specific area, jump to the relevant chapter and use the actionable steps provided.
- **Continuous Improvement**: Personal finance is a continuous journey. Use this e-book as a reference guide, revisiting chapters as your financial situation evolves.

Real-Life Success Stories

Throughout this e-book, you will find case studies and success stories of individuals who have achieved financial freedom. These stories will provide inspiration and practical insights into how others have navigated their financial journeys.

The Road Ahead

Financial freedom is attainable with the right knowledge, discipline, and strategies. By the end of this e-book, you will have a clear roadmap to build wealth, create passive income, and achieve the financial freedom you desire. Remember, the journey to financial freedom is a marathon, not a sprint. Stay committed, continue learning, and take consistent steps towards your financial goals.

Disclaimer

I am not a certified financial planner, CPA, broker, or real estate attorney. I am simply a person who has researched and put these principles into practice. You need to find your own CPA, brokers, and attorneys who can guide you in the particulars covered in this book.

With this introduction, you're now ready to embark on a transformative journey towards financial freedom. Let's dive in and start building the foundation for a financially secure and independent future.

Chapter 1: Understanding Financial Freedom

Financial freedom means having sufficient income to cover your living expenses without having to work actively. It provides the liberty to pursue interests and passions without financial stress. This chapter explores:

Definition and Importance

Financial freedom is defined as the state where an individual has enough financial resources to live comfortably without having to rely on a traditional job. This freedom allows for more life choices and security, enabling individuals to pursue their passions, spend more time with family, and engage in activities that bring them joy without worrying about finances.

Importance of Financial Freedom:

- **Stress Reduction**: Financial stress is a significant cause of anxiety and mental health issues. Achieving financial freedom alleviates this stress.
- **Life Choices**: Financial freedom allows for greater flexibility in making life choices, such as career changes, starting a business, traveling, or pursuing hobbies.
- **Security**: It provides a safety net in times of emergency, such as job loss or unexpected expenses, ensuring that basic needs are always met.
- **Legacy Building**: It enables individuals to build and leave a financial legacy for their loved ones, ensuring their well-being in the future.

The Stages of Financial Independence

Achieving financial independence is a progressive journey that can be broken down into several stages:

1. **Financial Dependence**: At this stage, individuals rely on others (parents, spouse, or financial aid) to meet their financial needs.
2. **Financial Solvency**: This is the first step towards independence where individuals are able to meet their financial obligations and living expenses on their own.
3. **Financial Stability**: Here, individuals have created an emergency fund that can cover 3-6 months of living expenses, providing a cushion against unexpected financial challenges.
4. **Debt Freedom**: Eliminating high-interest debts, such as credit card balances and personal loans, is crucial. Being debt-free increases disposable income and financial stability.
5. **Financial Security**: At this stage, individuals have investments or passive income streams that can cover their basic living expenses, such as housing, food, and utilities.
6. **Financial Independence**: This is the ultimate goal where passive income fully covers all living expenses, allowing individuals to retire early or pursue their passions without financial constraints.
7. **Financial Abundance**: Beyond independence, this stage involves having more income than needed to cover living expenses, allowing for luxury spending, philanthropy, and substantial wealth accumulation.

Setting Realistic Goals

Setting goals is crucial for achieving financial freedom. Effective goal-setting follows the SMART criteria:

- **Specific**: Goals should be clear and well-defined. Instead of saying, "I want to save money," specify, "I want to save $10,000 for an emergency fund."
- **Measurable**: Quantify your goals to track progress. For example, "I will save $500 per month."
- **Attainable**: Set realistic goals that are achievable given your current financial situation. Avoid setting goals that are too ambitious, as they can lead to frustration.
- **Relevant**: Ensure your goals align with your overall financial objectives and life plans. Saving for a home down payment is relevant if homeownership is a priority.
- **Time-bound**: Set a deadline for achieving your goals. For example, "I will save $10,000 within the next 20 months."

Examples of SMART Financial Goals:

- Save $10,000 for an emergency fund within two years by saving $417 per month.
- Pay off $5,000 in credit card debt within 18 months by paying $278 per month.
- Invest $200 monthly into a retirement account to build a $100,000 nest egg in 20 years.

Steps to Setting and Achieving Financial Goals:

1. **Assess Your Current Financial Situation**: Understand your income, expenses, debts, and assets.

2. **Identify Your Priorities**: Determine what financial goals are most important to you, whether it's saving for retirement, buying a home, or eliminating debt.
3. **Create a Plan**: Develop a step-by-step plan to achieve your goals, including budgeting, saving, and investing strategies.
4. **Monitor Your Progress**: Regularly review your progress and adjust your plan as needed to stay on track.
5. **Stay Committed**: Consistency and discipline are key to achieving financial goals. Stay focused and motivated by celebrating milestones along the way.

By understanding the importance of financial freedom, recognizing the stages of financial independence, and setting SMART goals, you can create a clear roadmap to achieve financial security and abundance. This chapter lays the foundation for the strategies and tools discussed in the subsequent chapters to help you on your journey to financial freedom.

Chapter 2: Building a Strong Financial Foundation

A robust financial foundation is essential for wealth building. This chapter covers:

- Setting financial goals
- Understanding net worth
- Creating an emergency fund
- Importance of financial education

Setting Financial Goals

Setting financial goals is the first step in building a strong financial foundation. It involves defining what you want to achieve with your money, whether it's buying a house, saving for retirement, or building an emergency fund.

Example: SMART Financial Goals

Let's take an example of setting a SMART goal for building an emergency fund:

1. **Specific**: "I want to save $5,000 for an emergency fund."
2. **Measurable**: "I will save $5,000 by putting away $200 each month."
3. **Attainable**: "I can adjust my budget to free up $200 monthly by cutting discretionary spending."
4. **Relevant**: "Having an emergency fund is important to cover unexpected expenses."
5. **Time-bound**: "I will have saved $5,000 in 25 months."

By following the SMART criteria, your goal becomes clear and actionable. Every month, you can track your progress and adjust if necessary.

Understanding Net Worth

Net worth is a key indicator of your financial health. It is calculated as the difference between what you own (assets) and what you owe (liabilities).

Example: Calculating Net Worth

Let's say you own:

- A home valued at $250,000
- A car worth $15,000
- Savings and investments totaling $50,000
- Personal belongings worth $10,000

Your liabilities include:

- A mortgage balance of $150,000
- A car loan balance of $5,000
- Credit card debt of $2,000
- Student loans totaling $10,000

Calculate your net worth:

Net Worth= $250,000
 15,000

$$50,000$$
$$+\underline{10,000}$$
$$\$325,000$$

$$\$150,000$$
$$5,000$$
$$2,000$$
$$\underline{10,000}$$
$$\$167,000$$

$$\$325,000$$
$$\underline{-167,000}$$
$$\$158,000$$

By tracking your net worth over time, you can see how your financial situation improves and make informed decisions to increase your wealth.

Creating an Emergency Fund

An emergency fund is a crucial component of a strong financial foundation. It provides a financial cushion in case of unexpected expenses such as medical emergencies, car repairs, or job loss.

Example: Building an Emergency Fund

Consider a scenario where your monthly living expenses are $3,000. Try to save enough to cover 3-6 months of expenses:

Emergency Fund Goal: 3×$3,000=$9,000 to 6×$3,000=$18,000

To build your emergency fund:

1. **Start Small**: Begin by saving $100 each month.
2. **Automate Savings**: Set up an automatic transfer to a dedicated savings account.
3. **Increase Contributions**: Gradually increase your monthly savings as your income grows or expenses decrease.

Over time, your emergency funds will grow, providing you with financial security. If you lose your source of income, you will now have a cushion to give you time and breathing space to find another source.

Importance of Financial Education

Continuous financial education is vital for maintaining and growing your wealth. It helps you make informed decisions and stay updated with financial trends and tools. Modern technology provides a wealth of informative resources for you to research.

Example: Financial Education Resources

To stay informed and enrich your financial knowledge, consider the following resources:

- **Books**: "The Total Money Makeover" by Dave Ramsey provides practical advice on budgeting, debt elimination, and wealth building. While I have not followed every principle of his, I have used several of them to build my wealth.

- **Online Courses**: Websites like Coursera and Khan Academy offer courses on personal finance and investing.
- **Podcasts and Blogs**: Follow financial experts such as Suze Orman and Ramit Sethi for tips and insights.
- **Financial News**: Stay updated with financial news through reputable sources like CNBC, Bloomberg, and The Wall Street Journal (Politics aside.).

By continuously educating yourself, you can make better financial decisions and adapt to changing financial landscapes.

By setting clear financial goals, understanding and tracking your net worth, building an emergency fund, and continually educating yourself, you can establish a solid financial foundation. This foundation is essential for wealth building and achieving financial freedom. The next chapters will delve into specific strategies and tools to further strengthen your financial position and move closer to financial independence.

Chapter 3: Budgeting and Saving

Effective budgeting and saving are crucial for financial stability. This chapter explores how to:

- Create a realistic budget
- Track your expenses
- Implement the 50/30/20 rule
- Automate your savings
- Use savings apps and tools

Create a Realistic Budget

A budget is a plan that outlines your income and expenses over a certain period. Creating a realistic budget helps you manage your money effectively and ensures you live within your means. One of the quickest routes to poverty is to live constantly beyond your means. You cannot continually spend more than you make and stay afloat financially.

Steps to Create a Budget:

1. **Calculate Your Income**: Determine your total monthly income, including salary, freelance work, and any other income sources.
    - For example: If you earn $4,000 from your job and $500 from freelance work, your total monthly income is $4,500.

2. **List Your Expenses**: Break down your expenses into fixed (rent, utilities) and variable (groceries, entertainment) categories.

- Fixed Expenses: Rent $1,200, Utilities $200, Insurance $150
- Variable Expenses: Groceries $300, Dining out $150, Entertainment $100

3. **Set Spending Limits**: Allocate funds to each expense category based on your priorities and financial goals.

    - Example: Allocate $200 for dining out and $100 for entertainment per month.

4. **Review and Adjust**: Regularly review your budget and adjust it based on changes in your income or expenses.

Track Your Expenses

Tracking your expenses is essential to understand where your money goes and to identify areas where you can cut back. Dining out and entertainment are two areas that you can sacrifice, at least temporarily, while you are strengthening your financial situation.

Methods to Track Expenses:

1. **Manual Tracking**: Record your expenses daily in a notebook or spreadsheet. When you use a card, whether debit or credit, you are often not aware of how fast you are burning through money. Writing down you expenses puts them tangibly before your eyes.
2. **Apps and Software**: Use budgeting apps like Mint, YNAB (You Need A Budget), or PocketGuard to automate expense tracking. These are just some

examples of budgeting software. I am not endorsing any particular program. I have no financial interest or gain if you select one of these.
3. **Bank Statements**: Regularly review your bank and credit card statements to monitor your spending. Your statement reveals where your priorities lie. We always seem to find funding for what is most important to us.

Example: Using a Budgeting App

- Download the Mint app.
- Link your bank accounts and credit cards.
- Categorize your expenses (e.g., groceries, entertainment).
- Set budget limits for each category and track your progress throughout the month.

Implement the 50/30/20 Rule

The 50/30/20 rule is a simple budgeting framework that divides your after-tax income (and after charitable donations, if you wish to make any) into three categories:

1. **50% Needs**: Essential expenses such as rent, utilities, groceries, and insurance.

    - Example: If your after-tax income is $3,000, allocate $1,500 to your needs.

2. **30% Wants**: Non-essential expenses such as dining out, entertainment, and hobbies.

- Example: Allocate $900 to wants. This area can be flexible, or even eliminated if your situation calls for it. In many ways, it is still more cost effective to prepare and eat meals at home.

3. **20% Savings**: Savings, investments, and debt repayment.

    - Example: Allocate $600 to savings and debt repayment. Strive to pay more than the minimum payments on your debt.

Example Budget Breakdown:

- After-tax income: $3,000
- Needs (50%): $1,500
    - Rent or mortgage: $1,000
    - Utilities: $200
    - Groceries: $300
- Wants (30%): $900
    - Dining out: $150
    - Entertainment: $100
    - Hobbies: $50
    - Other: $600
- Savings (20%): $600
    - Emergency fund: $200
    - Retirement savings: $200
    - Debt repayment: $200

You should pay yourself at least as much as you pay in debt servicing.

Automate Your Savings

Automating your savings ensures you consistently set aside money without having to think about it. If it is removed from you account automatically and placed in a savings account, you will not feel the pain.

Steps to Automate Savings:

1. **Set Up Automatic Transfers**: Schedule automatic transfers from your checking account to your savings account.

   - Example: Set up a $200 transfer to your savings account on the first of every month.

2. **Direct Deposit Split**: If your employer offers direct deposit, split your paycheck to automatically deposit a portion into your savings account.

   - Example: Allocate 20% of your paycheck to your savings account and 80% to your checking account.

3. **Use Savings Apps**: Apps like Digit and Qapital can help automate small transfers to your savings based on your spending habits.

Use Savings Apps and Tools

There are numerous apps and tools designed to help you save money and manage your budget.

Popular Savings Apps:

1. **Mint**: Tracks your spending, helps create budgets, and offers financial insights.
2. **YNAB (You Need A Budget)**: Focuses on proactive budgeting and helps you allocate every dollar.
3. **PocketGuard**: Shows how much disposable income you have after accounting for bills and goals.
4. **Digit**: Analyzes your spending patterns and automatically saves small amounts.
5. **Acorns**: Rounds up your purchases to the nearest dollar and invests the spare change.

Remember, these are examples only. I do not receive anything financially if you choose to use one of these apps.

Example: Using Acorns for Automated Savings

- Link your debit or credit card to the Acorns app.
- The app rounds up your purchases to the nearest dollar and invests the spare change.
- If you spend $3.75 on coffee, Acorns rounds up to $4.00 and invests $0.25. This is like giving yourself a tip. It sounds small, but it adds up over time.

Keep in mind that these figures must be adapted for inflation. At the time of this writing, these numbers may seem unrealistic, but they are for illustrative purposes only. You must adjust them for your location. By creating a realistic budget, tracking your expenses, implementing the 50/30/20 rule, automating your savings, and using savings apps and tools, you can achieve financial stability and build a strong foundation for wealth building. The next chapters will delve into advanced strategies for debt management, investing, and generating passive income to further enhance your financial journey.

Chapter 4: Debt Management

Managing and reducing debt is a crucial step towards achieving financial freedom. This chapter delves into the nuances of debt management by exploring the difference between good and bad debt, effective debt repayment strategies, consolidation options, and tips for avoiding future debt.

Understanding Good vs. Bad Debt

Not all debt is created equal. Understanding the distinction between good and bad debt can help you make informed financial decisions. Good debt typically refers to borrowing that has the potential to increase your net worth or generate income. Examples include student loans, which can enhance your earning potential, and mortgages, which allow you to invest in property that may appreciate over time. On the other hand, bad debt usually involves borrowing for items that do not generate income or appreciate in value, such as credit card debt incurred from purchasing non-essential items or high-interest payday loans. Another example is car purchases. For most of us, operating a car or truck is essential. Just keep in mind that vehicles do not appreciate in value. A new car loses thousands of dollars in value as soon as you drive it off the lot. Recognizing these differences helps in prioritizing which debts to tackle first and which to manage strategically.

Debt Repayment Strategies

Effective debt repayment strategies can significantly reduce your financial burden. Two popular methods are the avalanche and snowball strategies. The avalanche method focuses on paying off debts with the highest interest rates first, thereby reducing the overall interest paid over time. This approach can save you money in the long run but requires discipline and patience.

Alternatively, the snowball method prioritizes paying off the smallest debts first, regardless of interest rate. It is called the snowball method because as soon as you pay off that first debt, you apply that money toward the second debt. This method provides quick wins and psychological boosts, motivating you to tackle larger debts. You keep adding to the "snowball" until you get to your largest debts, usually your car payment and your mortgage. Both strategies have their merits, and the choice between them depends on your financial situation and personal preference.

The challenge is to create a small margin in your finances that you can begin to apply to your debt load. Look for some expenses that you can eliminate or reduce to apply that to your first debt you want to pay off. Here is where you can make adjustments to dining out and entertainment. Skim some money here and apply it to your first debt.

Consolidation Options

Debt consolidation is another viable option for managing multiple debts. It involves combining several high-interest debts into a single loan with a lower interest rate, simplifying payments and potentially lowering monthly payments. Common consolidation methods include personal loans, balance transfer credit cards, and home equity loans. Personal loans can offer fixed interest rates and set repayment terms, providing clarity and structure. Balance transfer credit cards often come with promotional interest-free periods, which can be advantageous if you can pay off the balance within the promotional period. Home equity loans leverage your property's value to secure a lower interest rate, but they put your home at risk if you fail to make payments. Avoid car-title loans or payday loans if at all possible. They usually come with high interest rates, and you run the risk of losing your car. That would create another financial burden.

Understand that before you can obtain a title loan, you must have a clear title to your car. That means it is paid for already and worth more than the debt you are consolidating. That is so the bank or whoever is using it for collateral can sell it and pay off your loan. I personally used my car once for a consolidation loan, and the strategy worked effectively. However, the bank loan officer who made the loan advised me not to create more debt once my burden had eased slightly. I took his advice.

Understanding these options can help you choose the best strategy to streamline and reduce your debt.

Tips for Avoiding Future Debt

Preventing future debt is as important as managing current debt. Here is a summary of several tips mentioned above to help avoid falling into debt again. First, create and stick to a realistic budget that includes savings for emergencies. This ensures that unexpected expenses don't derail your financial stability. Second, build an emergency fund to cover at least three to six months of living expenses, providing a financial cushion against unforeseen circumstances. Third, use credit cards wisely by paying off the balance in full each month to avoid interest charges. Fourth, live within your means by avoiding unnecessary purchases and distinguishing between needs and wants. Finally, continuously educate yourself on personal finance to stay informed about effective money management practices and financial products.

By understanding the nature of debt, employing strategic repayment methods, exploring consolidation options, and adopting habits to prevent future debt, you can significantly enhance your financial health. This comprehensive approach to debt management lays a solid foundation for achieving financial freedom and building long-term wealth. The following chapters will guide you through investing basics, advanced strategies for building wealth, and generating passive income streams, furthering your journey towards financial independence.

Chapter 5: Investing Basics

Disclaimer: I am not a certified financial planner or advisor. I am not a broker of any kind. I am simply relating what has worked for me. You must seek your own advice with a trusted broker, advisor, or CPA.

Investing is essential for growing your wealth and securing your financial future. This chapter covers the fundamental aspects of investing, including different types of investments, understanding risk tolerance and diversification, starting to invest with little money, and setting up a brokerage account.

Types of Investments

Understanding the various types of investments is the first step in building a robust investment portfolio. The main types of investments include stocks, bonds, mutual funds, and exchange-traded funds (ETFs).

Stocks represent shares of ownership in a company and offer the potential for high returns but come with higher risk. **Bonds** are debt securities issued by corporations or governments, providing regular interest payments and lower risk compared to stocks. **Mutual funds** pool money from multiple investors to invest in a diversified portfolio of stocks, bonds, or other securities, managed by a professional. **ETFs** are similar to mutual funds but trade on stock exchanges like individual stocks, offering flexibility and typically lower fees.

By understanding these investment types, you can choose those that align with your financial goals and risk tolerance.

Risk Tolerance and Diversification

Assessing your risk tolerance is crucial when making investment decisions. **Risk tolerance** refers to your ability and willingness to endure market fluctuations and potential losses. Younger investors, with a longer time horizon, can generally afford to take more aggressive risks compared to those nearing retirement. Find a good broker and stay with that person for many years. he or she will work with you over the years and adjust your investment strategy as you near your retirement years.

Diversification is a strategy to manage risk by spreading investments across different asset classes, sectors, or geographies. This reduces the impact of any single investment's poor performance on your overall portfolio. For example, instead of investing solely in technology stocks, you might diversify by including bonds, real estate, and international equities. This is one of the purposes of mutual funds. They are invested in such a way as to help smooth out the highs and lows of market fluctuation. Diversification helps in balancing risk and reward, enhancing the stability of your investment portfolio.

How to Start Investing with Little Money

Starting to invest with limited funds is possible and important for building wealth over time. The earlier you start investing, the more successful you will be. Here are some strategies:

1. **Micro-Investing Apps**: Platforms like Acorns and Stash allow you to start investing with small amounts by rounding up your purchases to the nearest dollar and investing the spare change. Again, this is like tipping yourself.

2. **Fractional Shares**: Some brokerage firms, such as Robinhood and Charles Schwab, offer fractional shares, enabling you to buy portions of expensive stocks with minimal investment.
3. **Low-Cost ETFs**: Investing in low-cost ETFs provides instant diversification with small initial investments. Many ETFs have low expense ratios, making them cost-effective options for new investors.
4. **Employer-Sponsored Retirement Plans**: Contributing to a 401(k) or similar retirement plan offered by your employer can be an easy way to start investing, especially if your employer matches contributions. You should try to set aside at least what your company will match. If they offer to match three percent of your salary, you should invest that same amount, too. That is one way to get a guaranteed one-hundred percent return on your investment.

Starting small allows you to build the habit of investing and take advantage of compound interest over time. it works similarly to the snowball method of paying off your debt.

Setting Up a Brokerage Account

Setting up a brokerage account is a necessary step to start investing. This is why I suggested that you find a reputable broker. Here's how to get started:

1. **Choose a Brokerage Firm**: Research and select a brokerage firm that meets your needs, considering factors like fees, investment options, and user experience. Popular options include Vanguard, Fidelity, Edward-Jones, and TD Ameritrade to name just a few. No endorsement is implied here.

2. **Account Types**: Decide on the type of account you need. For general investing, a taxable brokerage account is suitable. For retirement savings, consider an IRA, Roth IRA, or an annuity that can offer tax advantages.
3. **Application Process**: Complete the application process, which typically involves providing personal information, employment details, and financial information. This can often be done online.
4. **Fund Your Account**: Deposit funds into your brokerage account via bank transfer, wire transfer, or check. Some brokers may offer promotions for initial deposits.
5. **Start Investing**: Once your account is funded, you can start purchasing investments based on your research and financial goals.

By setting up and funding a brokerage account, you gain access to the markets and can begin building your investment portfolio.

Investing is a powerful tool for growing your wealth. By understanding the types of investments, assessing your risk tolerance, starting with small amounts, and setting up a brokerage account, you can embark on your investment journey with confidence. The next chapters will delve into more advanced investment strategies and ways to generate passive income, further enhancing your path to financial freedom.

Chapter 6: Advanced Investment Strategies

For those ready to take their investing to the next level, this chapter delves into several advanced investment strategies, including active vs. passive investing, value investing, growth investing, dollar-cost averaging, and rebalancing your portfolio. These strategies can help enhance your investment returns and better manage risk.

Active vs. Passive Investing

Active investing involves frequent buying and selling of securities to outperform the market. This strategy requires substantial research, analysis, and a proactive approach to capitalize on market opportunities. Active investors often use technical analysis, market timing, and individual stock picking to achieve their goals. Although active investing can potentially yield high returns, it also carries higher risks and usually incurs higher fees due to frequent trading. You must be aware of the risks when taking this route.

In contrast, passive investing aims to match market performance rather than beat it. This strategy typically involves investing in index funds or ETFs that replicate the performance of a specific index, such as the S&P 500. Passive investing is generally more cost-effective, involves less trading, and provides broad market exposure. Over the long term, passive investing has been shown to be an effective strategy for most investors due to lower costs and reduced risk of underperformance. Some call this a "buy and hold" strategy.

Value Investing

Value investing is a strategy where investors seek to buy undervalued stocks that they believe are trading below their intrinsic value. This approach was popularized by Benjamin Graham and Warren Buffett, who focus on investing in companies with strong fundamentals, such as low price-to-earnings (P/E) ratios, high dividend yields, and robust financial health. Value investors conduct thorough research to identify companies that are overlooked or undervalued by the market, with the expectation that their stock prices will eventually rise to reflect their true worth. This strategy requires patience and a long-term perspective, as it may take time for the market to recognize the value of these investments.

Growth Investing

Growth investing focuses on companies that are expected to grow at an above-average rate compared to other companies in the market. Growth investors look for businesses with strong potential for expansion, innovative products or services, and significant market share gains. These companies often reinvest their earnings into the business rather than paying dividends. As a result, growth stocks can offer substantial capital appreciation but come with higher risk due to their often high valuations and reliance on continued strong performance. Key metrics for growth investors include revenue growth, earnings growth, and return on equity (ROE).

Dollar-Cost Averaging

Dollar-cost averaging (DCA) is an investment strategy where investors consistently invest a fixed amount of money into a particular investment, such as a stock or mutual fund, at regular intervals, regardless of the investment's price. This approach reduces the impact of market volatility by spreading out investments over time, allowing investors to buy more shares when prices are low and fewer shares when prices are high. DCA helps mitigate the risk of making large investments at inopportune times and promotes disciplined investing. This strategy is particularly beneficial for those who have a steady income and prefer a hands-off approach to investing.

This strategy has worked well for me. I began decades ago putting money into an annuity through my job. I also invested an inheritance through a broker, and that account has done well over the years. During times of major volatility, such as in 2008, we lost a great deal of money, however, it rebounded quickly.

Rebalancing Your Portfolio

Rebalancing involves periodically adjusting your investment portfolio to maintain your desired asset allocation. As market conditions change, the value of different assets in your portfolio can shift, potentially causing your portfolio to become more or less risky than intended. For example, if stocks perform well, their value might increase disproportionately compared to bonds, leading to an overexposure to equities. Rebalancing involves selling some of the overperforming assets and buying underperforming ones to restore the original asset allocation. This process helps manage risk and ensures that your portfolio remains aligned with your investment goals and risk tolerance. Rebalancing can be done on a regular schedule (e.g., annually) or when your asset allocation deviates significantly from your target.

By exploring these advanced investment strategies, you can enhance your ability to grow wealth while effectively managing risk. Active and passive investing cater to different styles and preferences, value and growth investing offer distinct approaches to stock selection, and techniques like dollar-cost averaging and portfolio rebalancing help maintain a disciplined and balanced investment strategy. The following chapters will further explore methods for generating passive income and building a diversified investment portfolio to achieve financial independence.

Chapter 7: Building Passive Income Streams

Passive income is crucial for achieving financial independence as it provides a steady cash flow with minimal ongoing effort. This chapter explores various methods to generate passive income, including dividend stocks, real estate crowdfunding, peer-to-peer lending, creating and selling digital products, and earning royalties from creative works.

Dividend Stocks

Investing in dividend stocks is a popular way to generate passive income. Dividend stocks are shares in companies that regularly distribute a portion of their earnings to shareholders in the form of dividends. Companies with a history of stable and increasing dividends, often referred to as "dividend aristocrats," are particularly attractive for income-focused investors. By reinvesting these dividends or using them as regular income, investors can build a significant passive income stream over time. Moreover, dividend stocks can provide the added benefit of capital appreciation, making them a dual-purpose investment for both income and growth.

Real Estate Crowdfunding

Real estate crowdfunding allows individual investors to pool their resources to invest in real estate projects that would otherwise be inaccessible due to high capital requirements. Platforms like Fundrise and RealtyMogul enable investors to buy shares in residential and commercial properties, earning passive income through rental yields and property appreciation. This method offers a way to diversify into real estate without the need to directly manage properties. Additionally, investors can choose from a variety of projects to match their risk tolerance and investment goals, whether they prefer stable income from rental properties or higher potential returns from development projects.

Peer-to-Peer Lending

Peer-to-peer (P2P) lending platforms such as LendingClub and Prosper connect borrowers with individual lenders, bypassing traditional financial institutions. Investors can earn passive income by lending money to borrowers and receiving interest payments over the loan term. P2P lending allows for diversification across multiple loans, spreading risk and providing a steady income stream. However, it is important to note that P2P lending carries default risk, and investors should carefully evaluate the creditworthiness of borrowers and consider diversifying across different loan grades and terms to mitigate this risk.

Creating and Selling Digital Products

Creating and selling digital products like e-books such as the one linked to this book, online courses, and software are excellent ways to generate passive income. Once these products are developed and launched, they can be sold repeatedly with minimal additional effort. For instance, an e-book on a popular topic can be sold on platforms like Amazon Kindle, generating royalties from each sale. I personally have several books on Kindle. You may have found this book there yourself. Similarly, online courses hosted on platforms like Udemy or Teachable can attract a global audience, providing ongoing income as new students enroll. Digital products leverage your expertise and creativity, offering scalability and the potential for significant passive income.

Royalties from Creative Works

Royalties from creative works, such as music, books, and patents, can provide a continuous income stream. Artists, writers, and inventors earn royalties whenever their work is sold, performed, or used. For example, an author receives royalties each time their book is sold, and a musician earns royalties when their song is streamed or played on the radio. Additionally, licensing patents or trademarks can generate royalties from companies that use your intellectual property. This form of passive income can be particularly lucrative if the creative work becomes widely popular or is used extensively.

By diversifying into multiple passive income streams, you can enhance financial stability and work towards financial independence. Dividend stocks, real estate crowdfunding, and peer-to-peer lending offer different risk and return profiles, allowing you to tailor your investment strategy to your goals. Creating and selling digital products leverages your knowledge and skills, while earning royalties from creative works can provide long-term income from your artistic or intellectual endeavors. The following chapters will delve into more advanced wealth-building strategies, ensuring a comprehensive approach to achieving financial freedom.

Chapter 8: Real Estate Investments

Real estate can be a powerful wealth-building tool, offering numerous avenues for generating income and building long-term wealth. This chapter explores various real estate investment strategies, including buying rental properties, investing in real estate investment trusts (REITs), house hacking, short-term rentals like Airbnb, and commercial real estate.

Buying Rental Properties

Buying rental properties is a traditional and popular form of real estate investment. This strategy involves purchasing residential properties to rent out to tenants, providing a steady stream of rental income. Successful rental property investments require thorough market research to identify properties in desirable locations with strong rental demand. Additionally, investors must consider property management responsibilities, including maintenance, tenant screening, and rent collection. With proper management and a good location, rental properties can offer consistent cash flow and potential appreciation over time, contributing significantly to wealth building.

We use local property management companies to handle our rental properties. They screened the tenants, inspected the property, and made repairs that we authorized and paid for, and dealt with rent collections. We did not make as much off the rent as we would have had we done the work ourselves, but it was worth the price not to face the hassle of property management.

Real Estate Investment Trusts (REITs)

Real Estate Investment Trusts (REITs) offer a way to invest in real estate without owning physical properties. REITs are companies that own, operate, or finance income-producing real estate across various sectors, including residential, commercial, and industrial. By purchasing shares of a REIT, investors can earn dividends generated from the income produced by the real estate holdings. REITs provide liquidity similar to stocks, allowing investors to buy and sell shares on major exchanges. They also offer diversification, as REITs typically invest in a portfolio of properties. This makes REITs an attractive option for those looking to gain exposure to real estate with lower capital requirements and reduced management responsibilities.

House Hacking

House hacking is a strategy where investors buy a property, live in one part of it, and rent out the remaining space to generate income. Common examples include purchasing a duplex, triplex, or fourplex, living in one unit, and renting out the others. This approach can significantly reduce or eliminate housing costs, as rental income can cover mortgage payments and other expenses.

House hacking is particularly beneficial for first-time investors, as it provides hands-on experience in property management while offering the financial benefits of rental income. It also allows for low down payments and favorable loan terms typically associated with primary residences.

Short-Term Rentals (Airbnb)

Short-term rentals, facilitated by platforms like Airbnb, offer another lucrative real estate investment opportunity. This strategy involves renting out properties on a short-term basis to travelers and tourists. Short-term rentals can generate higher rental income compared to long-term leases, especially in popular tourist destinations or urban areas. However, managing short-term rentals requires more effort, including frequent cleaning, guest communication, and property maintenance. Additionally, investors must stay informed about local regulations and market trends, as some areas have restrictions on short-term rentals. Despite these challenges, short-term rentals can be highly profitable and provide significant cash flow.

I have been looking into investing in vacation properties to rent out and cover the costs. I had a neighbor who owned three cabins in the mountains just a few hours by car from where we lived. The rentals paid for his costs. When he wanted to go, he simply blocked out that time for his own use. That way he could go whenever he wanted.

Commercial Real Estate

Investing in commercial real estate involves purchasing properties used for business purposes, such as office buildings, retail centers, industrial warehouses, and multifamily apartment complexes. Commercial real estate can offer substantial income through lease agreements with businesses, often resulting in long-term, stable rental income. These properties typically yield higher returns compared to residential real estate but require more significant capital investment and expertise. Commercial real estate investments are influenced by economic conditions, market demand, and location. Investors often engage in thorough due diligence, including analyzing lease terms, tenant quality, and property condition. Commercial real estate can be a valuable addition to a diversified investment portfolio, providing income, appreciation potential, and tax benefits.

By understanding and leveraging these various real estate investment strategies, investors can build substantial wealth and achieve financial independence. Whether through buying rental properties, investing in REITs, house hacking, managing short-term rentals, or venturing into commercial real estate, each approach offers unique benefits and opportunities for income generation and portfolio diversification. The subsequent chapters will continue to explore advanced financial strategies, ensuring a comprehensive approach to wealth building and financial freedom.

Chapter 9: Stock Market Investments

Investing in the stock market can yield high returns and is an essential component of a diversified investment strategy. This chapter explores various aspects of stock market investments, including stock picking vs. index funds, understanding stock market cycles, reading financial statements, using stock screeners, and dividend investing.

Stock Picking vs. Index Funds

One of the primary decisions investors face is whether to engage in stock picking or invest in index funds. **Stock picking** involves selecting individual stocks based on research, analysis, and personal judgment. This strategy can lead to high returns if the chosen stocks perform well, but it also carries higher risk due to the potential for poor stock performance and lack of diversification. Successful stock picking requires substantial time and expertise in analyzing market trends and company fundamentals.

In contrast, **index funds** are mutual funds or ETFs that replicate the performance of a specific market index, such as the S&P 500. Investing in index funds offers diversification, as these funds hold a broad range of stocks within the index. This strategy is generally lower risk and requires less active management compared to stock picking. Index funds are also known for their low fees and consistent performance over time, making them an attractive option for long-term investors seeking steady growth.

Understanding Stock Market Cycles

Understanding stock market cycles is crucial for making informed investment decisions. The stock market goes through **cycles of expansion and contraction** influenced by economic conditions, interest rates, and investor sentiment. **Bull markets** are characterized by rising stock prices and investor optimism, while **bear markets** involve declining stock prices and widespread pessimism. Recognizing these cycles helps investors time their investments, though predicting market movements precisely is challenging. Knowledge of historical trends and economic indicators can provide insights into current market conditions, helping investors adjust their strategies accordingly.

Remember, I am neither a broker nor an advisor. This is for educational purposes only.

Reading Financial Statements

Reading and interpreting **financial statements** is essential for evaluating a company's performance and making informed investment choices. The three primary financial statements are the **income statement, balance sheet**, and **cash flow statement**. The income statement shows a company's revenue, expenses, and profits over a specific period, indicating its profitability. The balance sheet provides a snapshot of a company's assets, liabilities, and shareholders' equity, reflecting its financial health. The cash flow statement details the inflows and outflows of cash, revealing the company's liquidity and cash management. Mastering the analysis of these statements allows investors to assess a company's financial stability and growth potential.

Using Stock Screeners

Stock screeners are powerful tools that help investors filter and identify stocks based on specific criteria. These online tools allow users to set parameters such as market capitalization, P/E ratio, dividend yield, and sector. By inputting these criteria, investors can generate a list of stocks that meet their investment goals and risk tolerance. Stock screeners save time and enhance decision-making by providing a focused selection of potential investment opportunities. Popular stock screeners include those offered by Yahoo Finance, Finviz, and TradingView.

Dividend Investing

Dividend investing focuses on purchasing stocks that pay regular dividends, providing a steady stream of passive income. Dividend stocks are often from well-established companies with stable earnings and a history of distributing profits to shareholders. This strategy appeals to investors seeking income in addition to potential capital gains. Key metrics for evaluating dividend stocks include the dividend yield, payout ratio, and dividend growth rate. Reinvesting dividends through a dividend reinvestment plan (DRIP) can further compound returns over time. Dividend investing not only offers income but also adds a level of stability to an investment portfolio.

By understanding these core aspects of stock market investments, investors can make more informed decisions and tailor their strategies to their financial goals and risk tolerance. Stock picking versus index funds presents a fundamental choice between active and passive investing. Understanding market cycles, mastering financial statement analysis, utilizing stock screeners, and focusing on dividend stocks are essential skills that can significantly enhance investment outcomes. The subsequent chapters will continue to explore additional investment strategies and wealth-building techniques, further guiding readers towards financial freedom.

Chapter 10: Alternative Investments

Diversifying your investments can significantly enhance returns and mitigate risks by spreading exposure across different asset classes. This chapter explores various alternative investments, including cryptocurrencies, commodities, collectibles, private equity, and hedge funds.

Cryptocurrencies

Cryptocurrencies have emerged as a prominent alternative investment class, characterized by digital currencies such as Bitcoin, Ethereum, and numerous altcoins. These digital assets operate on blockchain technology, offering decentralized and secure transactions. Cryptocurrencies can provide substantial returns due to their high volatility and potential for rapid appreciation. However, they also carry significant risks, including regulatory uncertainties, market volatility, and security concerns. Investors interested in cryptocurrencies should conduct thorough research, understand the technology behind them, and be prepared for potential losses. Diversifying within the cryptocurrency space by investing in different coins can also help manage risk.

Commodities (Gold, Silver)

Investing in commodities like gold and silver has long been considered a hedge against inflation and economic uncertainty. These precious metals have intrinsic value and tend to retain purchasing power over time. Gold, in particular, is often viewed as a safe-haven asset during market turbulence. Commodities can be purchased directly in physical form, through commodity-focused mutual funds, ETFs, or futures contracts. While commodities can stabilize a portfolio, they typically do not provide income and their prices can be influenced by a range of factors, including geopolitical events, supply and demand dynamics, and currency fluctuations.

Collectibles (Art, Wine)

Collectibles such as art and wine represent another form of alternative investment. These tangible assets can appreciate significantly over time, especially if they are rare, of high quality, or have historical significance. Investing in art requires knowledge of artists, art history, and market trends, while wine investing involves understanding vintages, regions, and storage conditions. Collectibles can provide substantial returns and also offer the added enjoyment of owning aesthetically pleasing or culturally valuable items. However, they are illiquid and their value can be subjective and influenced by trends and collector demand. Professional appraisals and auctions are often necessary to buy or sell these items.

Private Equity

Private equity involves investing directly in private companies or buyouts of public companies, resulting in their delisting from public stock exchanges. This investment class provides opportunities for substantial returns through business growth, operational improvements, and eventual exits via sales or initial public offerings (IPOs). Private equity investments are typically illiquid and have a longer investment horizon, often requiring a commitment of several years. They also usually require substantial capital and access to exclusive investment opportunities. Investors should consider private equity as a part of a diversified portfolio, acknowledging the higher risks and potential for significant rewards.

Hedge Funds

Hedge funds are pooled investment funds that employ a variety of strategies to earn active returns for their investors. These strategies can include leveraging, short selling, and using derivatives, aiming to generate high returns regardless of market conditions. Hedge funds are known for their sophisticated and aggressive investment techniques, often seeking to outperform traditional investment benchmarks. They cater primarily to high-net-worth individuals and institutional investors due to high minimum investment requirements and fee structures that typically include both management and performance fees. While hedge funds can offer high returns, they also carry substantial risks and may lack transparency.

By incorporating alternative investments into your portfolio, you can achieve greater diversification, reduce overall risk, and potentially enhance returns. Cryptocurrencies, commodities, collectibles, private equity, and hedge funds each offer unique advantages and challenges. Understanding these investment classes and their role within a diversified portfolio is crucial for achieving long-term financial goals. The following chapters will continue to explore advanced strategies and insights for wealth building and financial freedom.

Chapter 11: Tax Strategies for Investors

Effective tax planning can save you significant amounts of money and enhance your overall investment returns. This chapter covers key tax strategies for investors, including tax-advantaged accounts, capital gains tax strategies, tax-loss harvesting, and estate planning.

Tax-Advantaged Accounts (IRAs, 401(k)s)

Tax-advantaged accounts such as Individual Retirement Accounts (IRAs) and 401(k)s offer powerful ways to save for retirement while reducing your current tax burden. Contributions to traditional IRAs and 401(k)s are often tax-deductible, which can lower your taxable income for the year you make the contribution. Additionally, the investments within these accounts grow tax-deferred, meaning you won't pay taxes on the earnings until you withdraw the funds during retirement. Roth IRAs and Roth 401(k)s, on the other hand, are funded with after-tax dollars, but qualified withdrawals in retirement are tax-free. This can be particularly beneficial if you expect to be in a higher tax bracket in the future. Understanding the differences between these accounts and strategically using them can maximize your tax savings and retirement funds.

Capital Gains Tax Strategies

Capital gains taxes are levied on the profit from the sale of assets such as stocks, bonds, and real estate. Long-term capital gains, which apply to assets held for more than a year, are generally taxed at a lower rate than short-term capital gains, which apply to assets held for a year or less and are taxed as ordinary income. To minimize capital gains taxes, investors can employ strategies such as holding investments for longer periods to benefit from the lower long-term rates. Another approach is to strategically realize gains in years when your income is lower, thereby reducing your overall tax liability. Additionally, taking advantage of the annual exclusion for capital gains and using tax-advantaged accounts to hold appreciating assets can further reduce the tax burden.

Tax-Loss Harvesting

Tax-loss harvesting is a strategy where investors sell securities at a loss to offset capital gains from other investments. This can effectively reduce your taxable income for the year. For instance, if you have a capital gain from one stock, selling another stock at a loss can offset that gain, potentially resulting in zero taxable capital gains. The IRS allows you to use up to $3,000 of capital losses to offset ordinary income each year, with any excess losses carried forward to future years. It's important to be aware of the "wash sale" rule, which disallows the deduction of a loss if you repurchase the same or a substantially identical security within 30 days before or after the sale.

Estate Planning

Estate planning involves preparing for the transfer of your assets after death and can play a critical role in tax planning. Strategies such as gifting assets during your lifetime, setting up trusts, and utilizing the estate tax exemption can minimize the tax burden on your heirs. For example, the annual gift tax exclusion allows you to give a certain amount to each recipient tax-free each year. Trusts, such as irrevocable life insurance trusts or charitable remainder trusts, can also help manage estate taxes and ensure your assets are distributed according to your wishes. Proper estate planning not only helps reduce taxes but also provides peace of mind by ensuring your financial legacy is protected and transferred smoothly.

This is where you will need to consult professionals. Inheritance and tax laws can vary from state to state.

By implementing these tax strategies, investors can significantly enhance their after-tax returns and preserve more of their wealth. Utilizing tax-advantaged accounts, strategically managing capital gains, engaging in tax-loss harvesting, and effective estate planning are essential components of a comprehensive tax strategy. The following chapters will continue to explore additional methods for building and preserving wealth, guiding readers towards achieving financial freedom.

Chapter 12: Retirement Planning

Planning for retirement is crucial for ensuring a secure and comfortable future. This chapter delves into various aspects of retirement planning, including different retirement accounts, calculating retirement needs, Social Security benefits, annuities, and withdrawal strategies.

Different Retirement Accounts (Traditional vs. Roth IRA)

Understanding the types of retirement accounts available is a fundamental step in retirement planning. **Traditional IRAs** allow individuals to contribute pre-tax income, which can grow tax-deferred until withdrawal. This means you won't pay taxes on the contributions or earnings until you retire and start taking distributions, potentially when you're in a lower tax bracket. **Roth IRAs**, on the other hand, are funded with after-tax dollars, but qualified withdrawals during retirement are tax-free. This can be advantageous if you expect to be in a higher tax bracket in the future. Deciding between a Traditional IRA and a Roth IRA depends on your current income, expected future income, and tax considerations.

Calculating Retirement Needs

Calculating how much money you will need for retirement is essential for effective planning. This involves estimating your future living expenses, healthcare costs, lifestyle choices, and inflation. A common rule of thumb is to aim for 70-80% of your pre-retirement income to maintain your standard of living in retirement. Tools like retirement calculators can help you determine how much you need to save based on your desired retirement age, expected lifespan, and current savings. Regularly reviewing and adjusting these estimates as you approach retirement can ensure that you stay on track to meet your goals.

Social Security Benefits

Social Security benefits are a critical component of most retirement plans. Understanding how Social Security works and how to maximize your benefits is essential. The amount you receive is based on your earnings history and the age at which you start claiming benefits. Delaying benefits past your full retirement age can increase your monthly payment, while claiming early can reduce it. Strategizing the timing of your Social Security benefits can significantly impact your overall retirement income. It's also important to consider how Social Security integrates with your other retirement savings and income sources.

At this writing, I still need a little over a year to receive my full benefits, so I will need to work a while longer. Depending on Social Security alone is not a wise option. Politics can affect what it pays out, plus it will not give you nearly enough to live on by itself without some other source of income such as a separate retirement account.

Annuities

Annuities are financial products that provide a steady income stream, typically for life, in exchange for an initial lump sum payment. They can be a useful tool for ensuring you don't outlive your savings. There are various types of annuities, including fixed, variable, and indexed annuities, each with different features and benefits. Fixed annuities provide guaranteed payments, while variable annuities offer payments that can vary based on the performance of underlying investments. Indexed annuities offer returns linked to a stock market index. Understanding the fees, terms, and potential benefits of annuities is crucial before incorporating them into your retirement plan.

Withdrawal Strategies

Developing a withdrawal strategy is vital to ensure that your retirement savings last throughout your retirement years. A common approach is the **4% rule**, which suggests withdrawing 4% of your retirement savings in the first year of retirement and adjusting that amount for inflation each subsequent year. This method aims to provide a steady income while preserving your principal. Other strategies include the **bucket strategy**, where assets are divided into different "buckets" based on when they will be needed, and the **systematic withdrawal plan**, which involves withdrawing a fixed percentage of your portfolio each year. Choosing the right strategy depends on your income needs, risk tolerance, and overall financial situation.

By understanding and implementing these elements of retirement planning, you can create a comprehensive plan that ensures financial security in your retirement years. Different retirement accounts, accurate calculation of retirement needs, strategic use of Social Security benefits, consideration of annuities, and effective withdrawal strategies all play crucial roles in building a robust retirement plan. The following chapters will continue to explore more advanced financial strategies, providing a roadmap to achieving long-term financial freedom.

Chapter 13: Protecting Your Wealth

Protecting your wealth is as important as building it. Ensuring that the assets you've accumulated are safeguarded against potential risks is essential for long-term financial security. This chapter covers critical aspects of wealth protection, including insurance, estate planning, trusts, legal protections, and identity theft prevention.

Insurance (Life, Health, Disability, Property)

Insurance is a foundational element in protecting your wealth. Various types of insurance provide financial security against unforeseen events.

Life insurance ensures that your dependents are financially supported in the event of your death, covering expenses such as mortgages, education, and daily living costs.

Health insurance protects against high medical expenses, ensuring you have access to necessary healthcare without depleting your savings.

Disability insurance provides income replacement if you become unable to work due to illness or injury, maintaining your financial stability during periods of incapacity.

Property insurance safeguards your assets, including your home and personal belongings, against damages from natural disasters, theft, and other hazards. Having adequate insurance coverage is crucial to mitigate risks and prevent financial loss.

Estate Planning

Estate planning involves preparing for the transfer of your assets upon your death, ensuring that your wealth is distributed according to your wishes while minimizing tax liabilities. A comprehensive estate plan includes a **will**, which outlines how your assets should be distributed, and designates guardians for any minor children. Additionally, **power of attorney** documents designate individuals to make financial and healthcare decisions on your behalf if you become incapacitated. Proper estate planning helps avoid probate, reduces estate taxes, and ensures a smooth transition of assets to your beneficiaries, providing peace of mind for you and your loved ones.

Trusts

Trusts are legal arrangements that allow you to transfer assets to a trustee, who manages them for the benefit of your beneficiaries. Trusts offer several advantages, including privacy, as they do not go through probate, and control, allowing you to specify how and when your assets are distributed. There are different types of trusts, such as **revocable trusts**, which can be altered during your lifetime, and **irrevocable trusts**, which cannot be changed but offer greater tax benefits and protection from creditors. Special types of trusts, like **charitable remainder trusts** or **special needs trusts**, serve specific purposes, such as providing for charitable donations or supporting beneficiaries with disabilities. Trusts are powerful tools in estate planning, enhancing asset protection and ensuring your wealth is managed and distributed according to your intentions.

Legal Protections

Legal protections encompass various strategies to shield your assets from potential lawsuits and creditors. **Asset protection planning** involves structuring your assets in ways that make them less vulnerable to legal claims. This can include forming **limited liability companies (LLCs)** or **family limited partnerships (FLPs)**, which separate personal assets from business liabilities, reducing your exposure to legal risks. Additionally, utilizing **homestead exemptions** and **retirement accounts** can protect certain assets from creditors. Consulting with a legal professional who specializes in asset protection can help you implement strategies tailored to your specific needs, ensuring your wealth is shielded from potential legal challenges.

Identity Theft Prevention

Identity theft can have devastating financial consequences, making prevention a critical component of protecting your wealth. Measures to protect your identity include **monitoring your credit reports regularly**, using **strong, unique passwords** for online accounts, and **enabling two-factor authentication** wherever possible. Be cautious about sharing personal information, both online and offline, and consider subscribing to **identity theft protection services**, which can alert you to suspicious activities and assist in recovery if your identity is compromised. Safeguarding your personal information helps prevent unauthorized access to your financial accounts and protects your wealth from fraudsters.

Check your credit card statements regularly and look for potential fraudulent charges. Make sure your bank and other financial institutions have fraud protection services. Once I received a phone call while I was in Peru. The bank wanted to know if I had authorized my card for home delivery pizza. "From Peru?" I asked. Obviously, I hadn't. I don't know any company that delivers to Peru!

By focusing on these areas of wealth protection, you can ensure that your financial assets are secure against various risks. Adequate insurance, comprehensive estate planning, the strategic use of trusts, legal protections, and proactive identity theft prevention are all essential components of a robust wealth protection strategy. The following chapters will continue to build on these concepts, providing further insights and strategies to help you achieve long-term financial security and freedom.

Chapter 14: Case Studies of Financial Success

Real-life examples of financial success can serve as powerful inspiration and guidance for those on their own financial journeys. This chapter features stories of individuals who have achieved financial freedom, detailing their strategies, mistakes, and the valuable lessons they learned along the way.

Stories of Individuals Who Achieved Financial Freedom

Learning from the experiences of others can provide valuable insights into effective financial strategies. One notable example is the story of Warren Buffett, one of the most successful investors of all time. Buffett's journey to financial freedom began with his early investment in stocks and his disciplined approach to value investing. By focusing on long-term investments and avoiding unnecessary risks, Buffett built a substantial fortune. Similarly, the story of Chris Reining, a former IT professional who retired at 37, highlights the power of frugality and strategic investing. Reining achieved financial freedom by meticulously saving over half of his income and investing in a diversified portfolio of stocks and real estate.

Their Strategies and Mistakes

These successful individuals employed a variety of strategies to build and protect their wealth. Warren Buffett, for instance, emphasizes the importance of investing in companies with strong fundamentals and holding onto those investments for the long term. His approach underscores the value of patience and thorough research in investment decisions. On the other hand, Chris Reining focused on aggressive saving and investing early in his career. He utilized tax-advantaged accounts, automated his savings, and lived well below his means to accumulate substantial wealth.

Despite their successes, these individuals also made mistakes that offer valuable lessons. Buffett has openly discussed his regrets about not investing in certain technology companies earlier and some of his less successful acquisitions. Chris Reining learned the hard way about the volatility of the stock market and the importance of not letting emotions drive investment decisions. By examining these mistakes, we can understand the importance of diversification, continuous learning, and maintaining a disciplined investment approach.

Lessons Learned

The experiences of these financially successful individuals provide several key lessons. First, the importance of starting early cannot be overstated. Time in the market often proves to be more critical than timing the market, as compound interest can significantly grow wealth over the long term. Second, living below your means and saving a significant portion of your income can create a strong financial foundation. This frugality, combined with smart investing, can accelerate the journey to financial freedom.

Another crucial lesson is the value of continuous education and adaptability. Successful investors like Warren Buffett and Chris Reining constantly learn and adapt their strategies to changing market conditions. They also stress the importance of keeping emotions in check and making rational decisions based on thorough analysis. Lastly, having a clear vision and set of goals helps maintain focus and motivation, ensuring that financial decisions align with long-term objectives.

By exploring these real-life case studies, readers can gain practical insights and inspiration for their financial journeys. The strategies, mistakes, and lessons learned from these successful individuals provide a roadmap for achieving financial freedom. The following chapters will continue to build on these concepts, offering more advanced strategies and tools to help readers secure their financial futures.

Chapter 15: Tools and Resources for Financial Planning

Utilizing the right tools and resources can significantly enhance your ability to manage your finances effectively. This chapter provides an overview of various financial planning tools, including financial planning software, budgeting apps, investment platforms, and educational resources such as books, courses, and blogs.

Financial Planning Software

Financial planning software offers comprehensive solutions for managing your finances, tracking your net worth, planning for retirement, and setting financial goals. Popular options include **Quicken**, which provides detailed insights into spending, budgeting, and investment tracking, and **Personal Capital**, which combines financial planning tools with investment management services. **YNAB (You Need a Budget)** is another excellent tool focused on proactive budgeting and financial goal setting. These platforms offer features like real-time account syncing, customized financial reports, and retirement planning calculators. By using financial planning software, you can gain a clear understanding of your financial situation and make informed decisions to achieve your financial goals.

Budgeting Apps

Budgeting apps are essential for tracking daily expenses and managing your budget effectively. Apps like **Mint** automatically categorize transactions and provide a visual overview of your spending habits, helping you identify areas where you can save money. **EveryDollar**, developed by financial expert Dave Ramsey, offers a zero-based budgeting approach that ensures every dollar is allocated to a specific expense or savings goal. **PocketGuard** simplifies budgeting by showing how much disposable income you have after accounting for bills and savings goals. These apps help you stay on top of your finances by providing alerts for upcoming bills, tracking spending patterns, and offering insights to improve your budgeting practices.

Investment Platforms

Investment platforms make it easier to start investing and manage your portfolio. **Robinhood** offers commission-free trading and a user-friendly interface, making it popular among new investors. **Vanguard** and **Fidelity** provide a wide range of investment options, including mutual funds, ETFs, and retirement accounts, along with robust research tools and financial advice. **Betterment** and **Wealthfront** are robo-advisors that create and manage diversified portfolios based on your risk tolerance and financial goals, offering a hands-off approach to investing. These platforms help you build and grow your investments, whether you prefer a DIY approach or professional management.

Educational Resources (Books, Courses, Blogs)

Continual learning is crucial for successful financial planning. Books like **"Rich Dad Poor Dad" by Robert Kiyosaki** and **"The Intelligent Investor" by Benjamin Graham** provide timeless insights into building wealth and investing wisely. Online courses from platforms like **Coursera**, **Udemy**, and **edX** offer structured learning on topics ranging from personal finance basics to advanced investment strategies. Blogs such as **Mr. Money Mustache** and **The Simple Dollar** provide practical advice, tips, and real-life experiences from financial experts and enthusiasts. These educational resources help you stay informed about the latest financial trends, strategies, and best practices, empowering you to make better financial decisions.

By leveraging these tools and resources, you can effectively manage your finances, make informed investment decisions, and continually expand your financial knowledge. Financial planning software, budgeting apps, investment platforms, and educational resources each play a vital role in helping you achieve and maintain financial health. The following chapters will continue to provide advanced strategies and insights, guiding you further along the path to financial freedom and wealth building.

Conclusion

Achieving financial freedom is a journey that demands a combination of knowledge, discipline, and persistence. By diligently following the strategies outlined in this book, you can take significant strides towards taking control of your finances, making wise investment choices, and building streams of passive income that pave the way for a secure and prosperous future.

The path to financial freedom is multifaceted, encompassing the fundamentals of budgeting and saving, smart investing, effective debt management, and proactive wealth protection. Establishing a solid financial foundation involves setting clear, achievable goals, understanding and tracking your net worth, and creating a reliable emergency fund. As you progress, mastering the basics of budgeting and saving becomes crucial. Implementing techniques such as the 50/30/20 rule, automating savings, and utilizing budgeting apps can help you manage your finances more efficiently and make informed spending decisions.

Investing wisely is another critical aspect of building wealth. By understanding different types of investments, assessing your risk tolerance, and diversifying your portfolio, you can grow your wealth over time. As you become more comfortable with investing, exploring advanced strategies such as dollar-cost averaging, rebalancing your portfolio, and focusing on passive income streams like dividend stocks, real estate, and digital products can further enhance your financial position.

Protecting your wealth is equally important. Adequate insurance coverage, comprehensive estate planning, the strategic use of trusts, and legal protections are essential to safeguard your assets from potential risks. Additionally, preventing identity theft through vigilant monitoring and security measures ensures that your hard-earned wealth remains secure.

The journey to financial freedom is not a sprint but a marathon. It requires ongoing learning, regular planning, and the ability to adapt to changing financial landscapes. Stay informed through educational resources such as books, courses, and financial blogs. Continuously review and adjust your strategies to align with your evolving goals and circumstances.

Remember, financial freedom doesn't happen overnight. It's a continuous process of learning, planning, and adapting. Celebrate your milestones along the way, stay committed to your goals, and keep pushing forward. With perseverance and the right strategies, you can achieve the financial independence you aspire to.

Good luck on your journey to financial independence! May this e-book serve as a valuable guide, empowering you to make informed decisions and take control of your financial destiny.

About the Author

Michael McGuire, Ph. D. is not a broker, CPA, or tax advisor or attorney. However, he is a successful parent, teacher, and author. He learned the principles of money management early in life and began to make financial progress.

In the beginning, and during the process of higher education, difficult times came, however, he has never filed bankruptcy, had any property repossessed or missed a meal that he did not miss on purpose.

Through the years, many have asked him to comment on his financial status. While not a millionaire (yet), he has shared his wisdom and experience in both formal and informal settings.

Michael has three grown children that he has taught these principles to. They are all successfully managing their lives and finances although they still have much to learn. His desire is that they will pass on this wisdom to their children as well.

Michael and his wife, Linda, live in west Texas.

www.ingramcontent.com/pod-product-compliance
Lightning Source LLC
Chambersburg PA
CBHW050019230526
45470CB00003B/1044